Spells to Attract Money

Simple, Powerful Money Magick for Everyone.

by

Rowan Wyldwitch

DISCLAIMER

This book is for informational purposes only. Whilst the author has made every attempt to ensure the information contained within is accurate, she makes no representation as to the accuracy, suitability or validity of the information contained within.

The author will not be held liable for any errors or omissions in the work and will not be liable for any losses, injuries or damages arising from its display or use.

Magickal results may vary.

Certain oils and botanicals may be hazardous to health. They should not be ingested or used directly on skin. Keep all such materials away from children and animals.

Burning candles can be a fire risk. Never leave a burning candle unattended or near flammable objects.

COPYRIGHT NOTICE

Copyright © 2016 by Rowan Wyldwitch

All rights reserved. This book or any portion thereof may not be reproduced or used in any manner whatsoever without the express written permission of the publisher except for the use of brief quotations in a book review.

CONTENTS

You Can Work Magick!
What is Magick?
   Magick and Karma
Preparing to Work Money Magick
Challenging Negative Thoughts About Money
How Do Magickal Spells Work?
1. Simple Candle Money Spell
2. The 50p Spell
3. Powerful Money Pouch
4. A Spell to Banish Debt
5. A Money Pomander
6. MOON HOODOO DOLLY MONEY SPELL
7. The Lucky Cookie
8. A Spell to Bring Success in Business
9. To Attract a Certain Amount of Money
10. Magickal Money Jar
11. Ancient Gypsy Money Spell
Easy Money Drawing Incense
Money Drawing Oil
FAST LUCK OIL (RED
MY SAFER ALTERNATIVE FAST LUCK OIL
Double Fast Luck Oil
Abundance Oil
   To Make Mint Extract
HERBS AND PLANTS WHICH ATTRACT MONEY

DAYS OF THE WEEK AND THEIR MAGICKAL CORRESPONDANCES

GEMSTONES WHICH ATTRACT MONEY AND INCREASE PROSPERITY

You Can Work Magick!

You CAN draw money into your life. In fact, you can do it right now. However desperate or bleak your present situation may seem, and however many times you have tried and failed, you can change your old ways of thinking about money in an instant. The principles I am going to talk about in this book never fail. They cannot fail, these are ancient universal laws as solid as the law of gravity. Gravity does not suddenly fail sending people flying off into outer space, and neither can the laws which govern the attraction of money fail. You do not need to understand metaphysics, quantum physics or indeed any sort of physics to understand the principles which are discussed here. Neither do you need an understanding of occult principles, you do not need to conjure up spirits and there is nothing "black" about this type of magick. The spells and rituals which you will learn about here are merely tuning into natural laws – laws which are as ancient as time and as unwavering as the universe.

Anyone can learn to use and harness the natural laws which govern magick. You do not need to dress up in a pointy hat or danced naked round a bonfire (unless of course you want to!). The traditional regalia of the magician and the props that many practitioners use to work magick are merely tools. Magick comes from within and we all have the power to use it as a tool to achieve our desires. However, in some of us our belief in magick and our ability to use it lies dormant as it clashes which other beliefs which we have accumulated on our life's journey. Beliefs that somehow magick is wrong or evil, or against religious principles can create a mental barrier stopping us from using this pure and natural power. Yet prayer itself is magick in one of its purest forms.

What is Magick?

Magick is a form of natural and neutral energy which we can learn to harness and use in our everyday lives. It is present in everything in the universe and all about us. We cannot see it, we cannot touch it yet we can learn to tap into it, to use its power for the greater good and to help us on life's journey. Magick is a neutral force, it is coloured only by the intent of its user. Magick can be used for good or bad purposes, just as electricity can be used to light a dark road so it's users can travel safely or to put a person to death. It should never be used to cause pain or harm to others however, and misusing its power in this way will not go unpunished. However, when it is used in times of genuine need, to help or to heal others it is benign and beneficial.

Magick and Karma

The law of attraction, that like attracts like is a well-known and universal law. If you have watched the very popular film "The Secret" you will understand the principles behind the law of attraction which also applies to Magick. If you use the neutral power of magick to do harm, to hurt others or force them to do your bidding, then you will only cause harm and pain to yourself. In Magick, we call this the threefold law of intent – any harm you cause to others will rebound on yourself threefold. Karma is another universal principle which states as you sow, so you shall reap. Magick is a very powerful force and its power should be respected. Ask for what you truly need, don't be greedy and respect other people's free will and magick will truly enhance your life.

Preparing to Work Money Magick

Money magick will help you in times of need. However, first you need to work through any negative beliefs you may be holding about money in general. Subconsciously, many people who find themselves with less than they need are holding deep rooted beliefs that money is somehow bad and that having money turns us into a bad person.

The idea that money leads to corruption and ruthlessness is perpetuated in society and in the media, from mean old Mr Burns in The Simpsons through to lottery winners who bemoan the very day fate smiled on them. Some of this deep rooted mistrust of money stems from the often misquoted passage from the bible that money is the root of all evil. Actually what the Bible says is "the love of money is the root of all evil" referring to avarice and greed.

Money, like magick itself is a neutral force, it can be used for the greater good such as giving to charity, funding projects like orphanages and improving the lives of others or for bad purposes such as building weapons of mass destruction, funding wars and destroying the lives of others.

If you believe that having money is inherently bad, or you do not believe you are worthy of money, even if those beliefs are lurking in the very depths of your subconscious, you will impede the flow of money to yourself, however hard you try to work money magick. The working and flow of magick is like a stream, if you stand downstream and let the water flow to you it will come naturally and easily. If however, you build a dam halfway down the stream then you will impede the flow. Some water may well trickle past the dam but the dam may also stop the water altogether.

Negative beliefs about money or indeed about magick act like a dam, they will stop blessings flowing to you until you take steps to remove them from your psyche. Have a deep and abiding trust that magick can – and will take care of it. Work through and abolish and negative thinking you may have about money. Once you have conquered these you will be hit by a tidal wave of blessings and good fortune. Ask and you truly shall receive.

Challenging Negative Thoughts About Money

If you are having a hard time convincing yourself that you are worthy of receiving money, you need to clear out all the negative thoughts you are holding in your subconscious mind and replace them with positive ones. If money is a constant source of stress in your life, if you are struggling to pay rent or bills then it can be quite difficult to stop the flow of negative thoughts surrounding money.

I once experienced these negative patterns of thinking and it stopped the flow of magick quite dramatically. At the time I was renting a very expensive house, my income started to dry up and I was really struggling to come up with the rent each month. Every day the postman appeared with what seemed like a new set of unpayable bills, so much so that even his approach would set off feeling of panic and anxiety. I couldn't afford to pay my fuel bills, I got behind with other debts and even the thought of money filled me with fear and dread. Not surprisingly, my magickal abilities suffered dramatically, my money spells produced very little results and the situation looked so grim I feared I would be evicted by my landlord.

In desperation I asked for inspiration and suddenly I realised that it was my negative thinking about money which was blocking money from coming to me. The answer involved a massive mind shift, from changing my thinking about lack to thoughts of abundance. No it wasn't easy, but I used the spells you will learn later in the book particularly the simple 50p money spell. I gave money to charity, I repeated affirmations of abundance, I refused to ponder on the negatives and focused on what I did have rather than what I did not. I visualised the postman bringing me positive news rather than negative and within a couple of weeks my situation had dramatically improved.

I received an unexpected windfall. I won a competition. My income once again started to rise. As the abundance started to flow it came faster and more easily. I had unclogged whatever psychic blockage I had developed towards money and once again it had begun to flow unimpeded.

Unfortunately, the human mind isn't like a computer which can be stripped down and the memory chip instantly replaced by another one. Some of our subconscious thoughts and beliefs really are resistant to change. However, did you know that your subconscious mind, which is where all those persistent thoughts and beliefs are stored cannot actually tell the difference between fact and fiction?

Our conscious mind is where we make judgements as to what is true or false, whereas the subconscious just passively receives all of the information we send it. The subconscious mind is nevertheless many times more powerful than the conscious mind. And if we want to erase deeply held beliefs, we need to speak directly to the subconscious mind. We can do this in many ways, by holding pictures in our mind, by repeating affirmations, by hypnosis, subliminal message software and by creative visualisation.

Just a simple affirmation such as "I am worthy of receiving money", "money flows quickly and easily to me" or "I attract abundance", can be very powerful in retraining your subconscious mind and unleashing the flow of money into your life.

How Do Magickal Spells Work?

Actually no-one actually knows exactly how spells work, but there is absolutely no doubt that they do. Magick, as we have discussed is a complex interaction between the mind and the environment design to bring about a certain outcome. It is an interplay of the laws of nature and the laws of attraction which manifests on the material plane. Magick is not mind power or belief alone, neither is it ritual alone, it is the synergistic interaction of the two which brings about a desired event. Magick is a powerful and ancient system of beliefs which has been closely guarded, passed down through generations and is still as alive and powerful today as it was in the beginning of time.

Virtually everything in the natural world has been endowed with some form of magickal attribute. The planets, days of the week and hours all have magickal correspondences, herbs and flowers are endowed with magickal properties and their use in spells and rituals will bring about certain results. These correspondences are still very much alive in everyday life, roses are associated with love and romance whilst yew, the tree of immortality, rebirth and transformation is often found in graveyards. Much of medicine has roots in ancient magickal and herbal remedies which proved in many cases to be more effective and less harmful than some modern alternatives.

When we study magick, we learn that these correspondences are not pure chance, they are a structured system based upon the principles that "like attracts like". This is also known as the law of sympathetic resonance, a physical scientific law which is often used as hypothesis to explain why magick works. If you place two pianos in a room and then strike a C note on one piano, you will find that the C string on the other piano will vibrate at the same time. This is known as sympathetic resonance. Using the same principle, when we carry out a magickal ritual in accordance with universal vibrations which align with that which you desire, you cannot fail to bring that which you desire about.

If delving into the laws of sympathetic resonance is a little too complex, don't worry. All you need to do is to believe that magick works for you and it will. Believe that the spells in this book will help you to attract the money you need and the money will come to you – as if by Magick.

Blessed Be

1. Simple Candle Money Spell

This is one of the simplest yet effective money spells ever. It is best done at the time of the waxing moon (when the moon is increasing in size) or during the full moon. Thursday is the best day of the week to carry out this spel .

YOU WILL NEED:

A new solid green candle, taper type is best. The colour needs to be solid all the way through, not a white candle which is dipped or coated in green wax. If you are unsure as to whether a candle is solid or not, nick it with your nail.

Something with a sharp point with which you can use to carve your candle. A biro pen is fine for this purpose.

Money drawing oil – see the recipes later in this book or make your own mixture of cinnamon, ginger and basil in a little olive or vegetable oil. If you have patchouli this will also work well.

Salt

HOW TO DO IT:

Firstly, prepare your candle. Wash it thoroughly to remove any negative influences, but be sure to keep the wick dry. Sprinkle over a little salt to further cleanse the candle.

Once the candle is cleansed, use your biro or sharp object to carve your desire into the candle. If you need a certain sum of money write this amount on the candle (remember not to be greedy) or if you want to increase the amount of money flowing to you then write something like draw money to me, or bring me wealth and prosperity. Take your time and carve every inch of the candle, fill up the empty spaces with symbols which represent money in your currency. As you carve, visualise your desire as vividly as you can.

Once the candle is prepared, anoint it with your money oil. Start at the centre as work towards the ends with long stroking movements. Again as you anoint the candle, visualise it working its magick and bringing you your desires.

Finally, light the candle. As the candle burns, visualise how you will feel once you have received your wish. Experience the elation you will feel once your wish is granted, knowing money is now on its way. Stare into the flickering flame of the candle, certain in the belief that will you receive your request. Continue for as long as you desire, then thank the universe for the money which will be coming to you, then let the candle burn out completely.

An alternative way of doing this spell is to repeat the burning of the candle on consecutive days. If you wish to do this, do not let the candle burn out fully but instead pinch out the candle or use a snuffer – never blow out a magickal candle. Repeat until the candle has fully burned out.

2. The 50p Spell

Giving away money when you want to receive money may seem like a contradiction, but this is a very effective spell based on the laws that like attract like. By being generous you will attract generosity and by sending blessings out into the cosmos you will receive blessings in abundance. As I live in the UK, I tend to do this spell with 50p coins as they have a fairly large surface area with which to write on – gold £1 coins also work well, being the colour of abundance, however being smaller they are trickier to write on. If you live in the States, then you could use $1 bills or if you live in another country with small denomination bank notes then these could be used instead.

YOU WILL NEED:

50p coins – I like to use nine coins, dollar bills or whatever currency you have to hand.
green felt tip pen.

HOW TO DO IT:

Cleanse the coins if you are using them in a solution of salt water, if you can use natural sea water that is perfect but any saline solution will do. If you are using bank notes, don't soak them but instead sprinkle them with either salt or a solution of salt water.

Take your felt tip pen and write on each of the coins – this part is quite tricky as writing on coins is an art to be mastered, if you are using bank notes then this will be much easier. Write words which give a blessing to the finder, such as "good luck", "happiness", "success", "prosperity", "abundance", "love" etc. As this spell works on the three-fold law of return, the more good wishes and blessings you send out into the universe, the more abundance you will receive in return

Once you have written your blessings on the notes leave them on a window sill or out in the open in a safe place where the moonlight will shine upon them.

The next day, the fun begins. Take your coins and hide each one in a place where it is likely to be found by someone who would really appreciate it, maybe near a school or where someone who is homeless may sleep. Have fun placing the money and imagine how pleased and delighted the finder will be.

Very soon, your generosity will be rewarded many times over.

3. Powerful Money Pouch

Money pouches, purses and conjure bags are used in many magickal traditions. In this spell, you will sew your own pouch, making the magick even more powerful.

YOU WILL NEED:

Green satin or green felt
Gold thread
A cinnamon stick or cinnamon powder
3 silver coins any denomination
Patchouli oil or patchouli herb
Tigers eye gem

HOW TO DO IT

Make a pouch by cutting two squares from the material and sewing three sides together with the gold thread. As you sew repeat the following:
3 times 3 and 9 times 9
Money and fortune will soon be mine.

Turn the pouch inside out so that the stitching doesn't show

Place the cinnamon, a few drops of patchouli oil or a pinch of the herb if using, coins and tigers eye into the pouch.

Take a long piece of the gold thread and wind it around the open end of the pouch 9 times and then knot to seal it.

Carry the pouch on your person and it will attract riches to you.

4. A Spell to Banish Debt

This spell is best done during the waning moon, which is the time between the full moon and the new moon. A couple of days before the new moon appears is known as the black or dark moon, and this is a very potent time to carry out spells related to banishing and getting rid of things you no longer want in your life. Although some practitioners believe that no magick should be worked during this time, many people still believe that this is the most powerful time to carry out this type of work.

YOU WILL NEED

A solid black candle
A stack of bills or red letters – if you don't want to use your real bills then make a photocopy of them or use old bills.
Nine black peppercorns

HOW TO DO IT

This spell is best performed outdoors unless you want to be chasing scorched peppercorns around your room. Light the black candle and visualise the stack of bills getting smaller and smaller until they disappear altogether. Next take the black peppercorns and toss them one by one into the flame of the candle whilst repeating

"Debt be gone
Trouble no more
Never again come to my door"

Know that very soon your debts will be gone.

5. A Money Pomander

Pomanders were traditionally used as air fresheners and decorative items. Back in olden times, citrus fruits were considered a luxury item and were associated with wealth and prosperity.

YOU WILL NEED:
An orange or other citrus fruit
Cloves
Cinnamon, parsley, sage and dried basil
Gold glitter or gold magnetic sand
A green ribbon for hanging.

HOW TO DO IT

Prick a symbol of a pound sign, a dollar sign, the currency you use in your country or indeed any other symbol which represents money to you. Insert a clove into each hole whilst saying "money is coming to me" as you insert each clove.

Roll the pomander into the cinnamon, parsley, sage and basil in turn. As you work visualise the pomander bringing money and good fortune into your life. Finally sprinkle with the gold glitter or magnetic sand.

Tie the green ribbon around the pomander and hang it in a doorway or window.

Optional:
To keep your pomander charged and bringing good fortune into your life "re-anoint" it with the herbs and glitter on the evening of each full moon.

6. Moon Hoodoo Dolly Money Spell

This spell should be started on the first night of the new moon.

YOU WILL NEED
Corn husks and straw with which to fashion a corn dolly
Green yarn
A silver or gold coin
A velvet cloth
Fast luck or double fast luck oil (see the recipes at the back of this book)
Traditionally dust from a graveyard would be used in this spell but this is no longer used.

HOW TO DO IT

On the evening of the new moon, fashion a corn dolly from corn and straw. If you are unaware of how to do this, there are many instructions on the internet on how to do it but it does not have to be elaborate, merely tie the straw around the corn husks to fashion a vaguely human shape. Place a silver coin into the belly of the dolly and secure everything with the green twine. Place a drop of the fast luck or double fast luck oil on its head, hands and feet.

7. The Lucky Cookie

Magick in its most basic form is just the transfer of energy and intent. Any object whatsoever can be charged with magick. In this case we use an object which most people will already have in their homes – an ordinary cookie or biscuit as we say in the UK. This is quite literally a good fortune cookie!

YOU WILL NEED

A plain cookie
Icing or decorations – optional

HOW TO DO IT

Basically all you are going to do is charge the cookie with magickal intent and then transfer it to yourself by eating it!

If you wish to decorate your cookie prior to this ritual then feel free – you could draw the object on your spell onto the cookie using icing or the edible cake decoration pens which are sold in baking stores. You could decorate your cookie with symbols which represent money or good fortune such as four leafed clovers, elephants, money Buddha's or anything which symbolizes your desire.

You don't have to decorate your cookie, this spell will work just as effectively if you just use a plain cookie.

Find a place where you can be alone and undisturbed for at least half an hour. If you want to light some incense or a candle do so. However, the most effective magick requires only the mind and concentration.

Hold the cookie in your dominant hand and burn your intention onto it using your mind. Focus all your energy on implanting your desire onto the cookie. Speak your intention out loud. If you feel a bit daft talking to a biscuit remember that everything in the universe, animate and inanimate consists of energy. Even the chair you may be sitting on or the laptop I am typing this on are at their essence nothing more than dancing atoms. Your intention can be imprinted onto anything.

If you don't believe this, consider how a microwave cooks food. You cannot see the microwaves but they work by agitating molecules within the food which creates heat. Your mind is just like a microwave. Your desire and your will can be transferred to another object with sufficient concentration and focus.

Continue to imprint your desire onto the cookie – 20 minutes is a good length of time to aim for. Some people visualise that they are burning words onto the cookie with their mind, others speak their intentions out loud or create a sort of chant, how you do this depends on what comes naturally to you. There is no right way or wrong way to create intent.

Once you are satisfied that you have transferred your will to the cookie, eat it! By consuming your charged cookie, you are transferring all the focused energy back to you, your desire is now effectively within you.

Know that as you consume the cookie, your desire will be fulfilled so long as what you are wishing for is within the laws of the universe. Your intent should never be to cause harm to another person as not only will this not be effective, you will also be held responsible for your intention to cause harm by the laws of karma.

8. A Spell to Bring Success in Business

This spell is particular effective if you are starting a new venture, however it can boost the fortunes of established businesses too. The principle is one of sympathetic magick – as you nurture and grow your seedling, so the fortunes of your business also increase. Basil is a herb which is associated with prosperity, wealth and success.

YOU WILL NEED
A small silver coin of any denomination.
The seedling of a Basil plant. Alternatively, you can obtain basil seeds and grow the plant from scratch. Growing the plant from seed is particularly appropriate if you are just starting a new business, as the seed germinates and grows so will your business.
A plant pot made from natural materials – plastic is not appropriate for this spell, use stone or terracotta.
Soil
Water from a natural source – a river, stream or rainwater
A purple candle
Something that represents your business – a business card or letter head is ideal. If you do not have these items yet just write down the name and address of your business on a piece of paper.

HOW TO DO IT

This spell is best done on a Thursday during a waxing moon. The waxing moon is associated with growth and expansion and Thursday is ruled over by Jupiter, the god of prosperity and business affairs.

Light the candle. Sit for a moment and meditate on what you would like to achieve. Be specific – don't just say I would like my business to grow or I want to make more money. Focus on achieving a specific goal such as I would like to attract x number of new customers by x (make this a realistic goal) or I would like to make x amount in sales by a certain date. Visualise your business busy and thriving, imagine new customers coming through the door and visualise your order book overflowing. See yourself as a happy and successful business person.

Take the silver coin and place it at the bottom of your plant pot. On top of the coin place your business card or the piece of paper with your business details on it. Fill the pot half way with soil if you are using a seedling or nearly to the top if you are using seeds. Plant the basil and fill the rest of the pot with soil.

Sprinkle the water into the pot until the soil is moist and say aloud.

"Lord Jupiter I ask for your help
Watch over this business and help it grow
Bring opportunity and success to me
And it harm none so mote it be"

Let the candle burn down. Place the potted plant on a sunny windowsill and nurture it. As it grows, so will your business.

Note: Basil is a herb which is associated with prosperity and success and it is reasonably easy to obtain but you could use another plant if you wish. Chamomile is associated with luck and prosperity as are alfalfa and Irish Moss. Marjoram helps to protect both your home and your business from bad luck and jinxes. Cinquefoil is relatively easy to grow from seed as is very effective at drawing money. This spell could be done on a larger scale by planting either a juniper or a honeysuckle in the garden.

9. To Attract a Certain Amount of Money

This spell is ideal if you need a certain amount of money to meet an unexpected bill or unforeseen expense. At one time just about everyone had a cheque book but in this age of digital currency paper cheques are rarely used any more. If you don't have a cheque book don't worry, you can find downloadable cheque templates online that you can print out. There is one on The Secret Law of Attraction website.

YOU WILL NEED:
A blank cheque from your chequebook or a print out of a blank cheque.
Cinnamon powder
Either patchouli oil or a money drawing oil.

There are two ways of tacking this spell so you can choose the version you think is most appropriate to your circumstances.

HOW TO DO IT

The first is for when you need a certain amount of money by a deadline – for example if you have an unexpected high bill or an expense you have not budgeted for. The second is for attracting general prosperity and abundance.

This spell must be done on either a new or waxing moon do not try to perform it if the moon is waning. If you have an emergency expense during the waning moon, try the spell for banishing debt instead.

Take your cheque. If you are doing the first version of the spell to attract a certain amount of money then fill in your name as the payee, the date which you need the money by and the amount of money you need to receive. Sign the check with love from the universe.

If you just want to attract general prosperity do not fill in the date on the check or the amount you wish to receive. Instead write PAID IN FULL in both of the boxes where you would write the amount of money the cheque is for. This not only shows gratitude for what you have already received but by the law of attraction sets you up to receive more abundance.

Once you have filled in your cheque sprinkle it with cinnamon (cinnamon is very effective for attracting money) and put a few drops of patchouli or money drawing oil on it.

You can either put your cheque in a prominent place where you will see it often or keep it in your purse or wallet. Know that money, fortune and abundance is on its way to you.

10. Magickal Money Jar

Many of us have a jar of coins in our homes, where we stash our loose change or any odd coins we find. It's amazing how quickly this coins can add up to a nice sum of money! This spell works on the same principle, you are going to create a magickal money jar overflowing with blessings and good fortune

Bay leaves have many magical uses – they are associated with wealth and prosperity but are also very powerful for "wish" magick. One of the simplest spells ever is to write your desire on a bay leaf and release it into the wind or the ocean. Bay leaves also bring psychic protection, so not only will your magickal money jar bring you blessings, it will also protect your home.

YOU WILL NEED

A jar with a lid
Nine coins of the same denomination
Nine leaves
A felt tip pen
Sea salt and water

HOW TO DO IT

This spell should be done over nine consecutive nights during the waxing moon. This is the time traditionally associated with growth and expansion.

Firstly, dissolve the sea salt in warm water and use it to thoroughly rinse out the jar. This will help to clear any negative influences.

Write your desire on one of the bay leaves. Meditate for a few minutes imagining you being showered with abundance and good fortune.

Then drop one of the coins into your jar imagine it multiplying many times over. A you drop in the coin say

*"Lady fortune smile on me
multiply blessings three times three"*

On the second night, repeat the steps above with the bay leaf and coin. Write the same wish you wrote on the first bay leaf – repetition is the key to success with this spell. Continue for the next seven nights.

You can continue to add coins to the jar from time to time if you wish. When unexpected money begins to appear, give some away. Ten percent is a good amount to donate to charity or a worthy cause. The more you give the more you will receive as is the way of the universe.

11. Ancient Gypsy Money Spell

This is a traditional gypsy money spell that calls upon the spirits of the Trinka Five, thought to bring good luck and fortune. The origins of the trinka five are unknown, this is a spell which has been passed down through many generations. However, it is thought that it could refer to the five elements – earth, air, fire, water and spirit or ether.

YOU WILL NEED:
A white candle

HOW TO DO IT

Light a white candle
Repeat out loud:
"Trinka five, Trinka Five
Ancient spirits come alive
Money come
Money thrive
Bless me spirits of the trinka five.

MAGICKAL OILS, INCENSE AND RECIPES

Easy Money Drawing Incense

You may already have most of the ingredients for this incense at home in your kitchen. Frankincense grains can be purchased at any occult, new age or church supplies store or online. Orange essential oil is also very easy to come by. Ready made money drawing incense can be quite expensive, so not only will you save money by making your own, it will also be more effective as you have hand made it and imbued it with your intention.

YOU WILL NEED

1 part cinnamon
1 part orange grind, finely grated
1 pinch of nutmeg
1 part star anise
2 parts frankincense
A few drops orange essential oil

HOW TO DO IT

Use a pestle and mortar to combine the cinnamon, orange rind, nutmeg and star anise. Sprinkle on the essential oil and mix in the frankincense. Burn on a charcoal block in a very well ventilated area.

Money Drawing Oil

This oil can be used for spells and ritual to attract prosperity, to anoint candles, in charm bags or to anoint paper money. Use a few drops in an oil burner to magically charge the atmosphere before working money magick.

YOU WILL NEED

50 ml base oil – sweet almond, olive oil or grapeseed oil

5 drops patchouli oil
5 drops cedar wood essential oil
1 drop vertivert oil
1 drop of ginger essential oil
1 drop of cinnamon essential oil

Add each of the essential oils to the base oil. Mix well. Decant into a dark coloured glass bottle preferably with a dropper. Label and store in a cool dark place. Shake before using.

Do not use oil directly on the skin and do not ingest.

Fast Luck Oil (Red) - **Extreme Caution Required** –
See My Non Toxic Recipe On Next Page

This is the traditional voodoo recipe for fast luck oil which is coloured a vivid red. The original oil was made using pure wintergreen oil which is very toxic so this recipe is included just for reference and **not recommended for use**. The original plants and botanicals which were used to dye the oil red have been substituted in most modern recipes by ordinary food colouring which is just as, if not more effective in achieving the vivid shade of red for which this oil is famed. None of the potency is lost by using food colouring.

YOU WILL NEED

Essential oil of cinnamon
Oil of Wintergreen (Caution very toxic)
Vanilla Extract or Vanilla Absolute
Red Food Colouring

Mix all the ingredients together and keep in a sealed container away from pets and children. Do not use on skin.

My Safer Alternative Fast Luck Oil

Essential oils are very toxic, particularly wintergreen oil which can kill if even small amounts are ingested. I have come up with a safer alternative which many people have remarked smalls just like a wad of folding money! As a bonus, many of you will already have all the ingredients you need at home.

YOU WILL NEED:

Vegetable oil or any base oil to use as a carrier.
Vanilla essence – as used in baking
Dried Cinnamon powder
Vicks Vapour Rub or a similar product.
Red Food Colouring

Melt the ingredients together in a double burner or a bowl over a pan of hot water until dissolved. Bottle and use to anoint folding money or as a substitute for fast luck oil.

Double Fast Luck Oil

Double fast luck oil is believed to have twice the potency of fast luck oil and always looks very impressive with its two-tone red and green appearance. It is actually quite easy to make at home. All you need is an oil based red fast luck oil such as my recipe for Safer Fast Luck Oil and a water based or clear alcohol (vodka) based green solution.

To make the green "oil" take botanicals which are traditionally associated with luck, money and prosperity such as basil, parsley, mint, sage and a four leaf clover if you can find one and steep them in water or alcohol. If the solution is not green enough for your liking, then you can add a few drops of green food colouring. Pour the red oil and then the green oil into a clear bottle or container. They should separate out to form a two-tone effect.

To use the oil, shake to mix.

Abundance Oil

This oil can take a little while to prepare due to the time taken to make the mint extract. If you already have mint extract handy or can obtain some then it can be prepared in a flash.

To Make Mint Extract

One cup of fresh mint leaves
Approx. 1 ½ - 2 cups of vodka

Rinse the mint and remove the stems
Crush the leaves between your fingers to help release the natural oil.
Place the mint leaves in a jar with a lid. Fill the jar with vodka ensuring that the leaves are fully covered. If they are not totally submerged they can rot and spoil the mixture.
Shake the jar well and leave in a cool dark place for around one month.
Strain the leaves and bottle the mint extract in an airtight container.

Rosewater can be purchased at many stores as it is an ingredient in Persian and Turkish cuisine. Alternatively, if you have access to fresh rose petals you can make your own.

To Make Rosewater
You will need:
1 cup of fresh rose petals
2 cups of distilled water or boiled filtered water

Rinse the rose petals well to remove any parasites or pesticides
Place in a pan with the water and gently heat. After around 20 minutes much of the colour of the petals will have transferred to the water. At this stage strain the rosewater into an airtight jar or container. Store in the fridge until ready to use.

For the Abundance Oil
YOU WILL NEED

5 drops of green food colouring
5 teaspoons of rose water
5 teaspoons of sweet almond oil
5 teaspoons of mint extract
5 teaspoons of honey
a pinch of powdered clove
a pinch of cinnamon
a pinch of ginger

Mix all the ingredients together in a glass bowl. Stir the mixture clockwise in order to increase the blessings which will be coming to you. The mixture may try to separate slightly but it will eventually come together. Decant into an amber or dark glass container and store in a cool dark place.

This oil is very versatile and can be used for any spell which requires a prosperity oil. Be careful though because it will dye fabrics, skin or anything else it comes into contact with!

Herbs and Plants Which Attract Money

Hyssop – ends poverty
Camomile – for luck
Allspice – attracts business and success
Basil – for money and prosperity
Cinnamon – for fast money
Dill – general good luck and good fortune
Cloves – bring good fortune into the household.
Mint – good fortune
Patchouli – manifests money
Squill Root – A powerful money drawer popular in voodoo
Alfalfa – brings good luck
Elderberries – brings general money and abundance
Juniper – protects against debt and loss
Irish Moss – a type of algae which is a popular ingredient in hoodoo bags and money sachets.

DAYS OF THE WEEK AND THEIR MAGICKAL CORRESPONDANCES

Monday
Colour – Silver/White
Planet – Moon
Metal – Silver
Magickal Influences: Healing, Cleansing, Family, Psychic Powers, The Home

Tuesday
Colour – Red
Planet – Mars
Metal – Iron
Magickal Influences: Courage, Conflict, Physical Strength, Competition, Politics, Leadership, Overcoming Obstacles

Wednesday
Colour – Purple
Planet – Mercury
Metal – Quicksilver
Magickal Influences: Communication, Travel, Education, Self-Improvement

Thursday
Colour – Blue
Planet – Jupiter
Metal – Tin
Magickal Influences: Honour, Strength, Prosperity, Business, Family Matters, Expansion, Growth, Masculinity

Friday
Colour – Green
Planet – Venus
Metal – Copper
Magickal Influences: Love, Women's Matters, Fertility, Sexuality, Relationships, Harmony, Emotions

Saturday
Colour - Black
Planet – Saturn
Metal – Lead
Magickal Influences: Overcoming Obstacles, Banishing, Removing Negativity, Endings, Divination

Sunday
Colour – Yellow or Gold
Planet – Sun
Metal – Gold
Magickal Influences: Health, Happiness, Joy, Prosperity, Protection, Success, Healing, Victory, Creativity

GEMSTONES WHICH ATTRACT MONEY AND INCREASE PROSPERITY

Green Aventurine – attracts money, good luck and fortune
Peridot – Increases wealth and abundance
Turquoise – Attracts love, luck and money
Tigers Eye – Powerful bringer of good luck and prosperity
Fool's Gold – Attracts money and luck into your life.

Finally, I'd like to wish you luck and love in all your magickal endeavours and may you achieve your true heart's desire. Be responsible in all your magickal work and remember to harm none.

Blessed Be.